MAPS

by Robin Nelson

first step nonfiction

Lerner Publications • Minneapolis

What does a map show?

MINNESOTA
IOWA
Equator
Hawaii (United States)
Pacific
Ocean
Continental boundary
International boundary
Continent
Country
State, territory
Ocean
Mountains
0
1580
1 inch stands for 1580 miles
Peru
Chile

Water

ROCKY MOUNTAINS
GREAT PLAINS
COLUMBIA PLATEAU
COLORADO PLATEAU
Great Basin
BITTERROOT RANGE
CASCADE
NEVADA
LLANO ESTACADO
EDWARDS PLATEAU
Mt. Rainier 14,410 ft. (4392 m.)
Mt. Whitney 14,494 ft. (4418 m.)
Mt. Elbert 14,431 ft. (4399 m.)
Denver
Los Angeles
Phoenix
Minneap
Kansas Ci
an Diego
Great Salt Lake
Lake Powell
L. Mead
Grand Canyon
Mojave Desert
Fort Peck Lake
Lake Sakakawea
Lake Oahe
Missouri
Yellowstone
Snake
Columbia
N. Platte
Platte
Colorado
Arkansas
Canadian
Red
Rio Grande
Gila
Pecos
Brazos
James

Mountains

Texas
Louisiana
Mississippi
Alabama
Florida
Georgia
South Carolina

States

Cities

Little Canada
Roseville
Maplewood
Rosedale Shopping Center
C. of C.
Co. Rd. C
Cervais Lake
Midland Hills
Co. Rd. B
Roselawn Av.
McCarrons Lake
Keller
Frost Av.
Lauderdale
Univ. of Minn. – St. Paul
Falcon Hts.
Larpenteur Av.
Como Reg. Pk.
Lake Como
Wheelock Pkwy.
Como Zoo
Conservatory
Municipal Stadium
Bandana Square Hist. Site
L. Phalen
Keller–Phalen Reg. Pk.
Hillcrest
Ivy Av.
W. Maryland Av.
Maryland Av.
St. Paul
Beaver Lake
Energy Pk. Dr.
Amtrak Depot
Hamline Univ.
Front Av.
E. 7th St.
E. Minnehaha Av.
W. Minnehaha Av.
University Av.
3rd. St.
Marshall Av.
HUDSON
Univ. of St. Thomas
Concordia Coll.– St. Paul
Battle Creek Reg. Pk.
Macalester Coll.
Summit Av.
St. Clair Av.
Randolph Av.
Highland Pkwy.
Coll. of St. Catherine
Highland Pk.
Montreal Av.
Lower Afton Rd.
Butler Av.
Lilydale
West St. Paul
LEXINGTON BR.
Hidden Falls–Crosby Reg. Pk.
Lock & Dam No. 1
HENNEPIN CO.
RAMSEY CO.

Roads

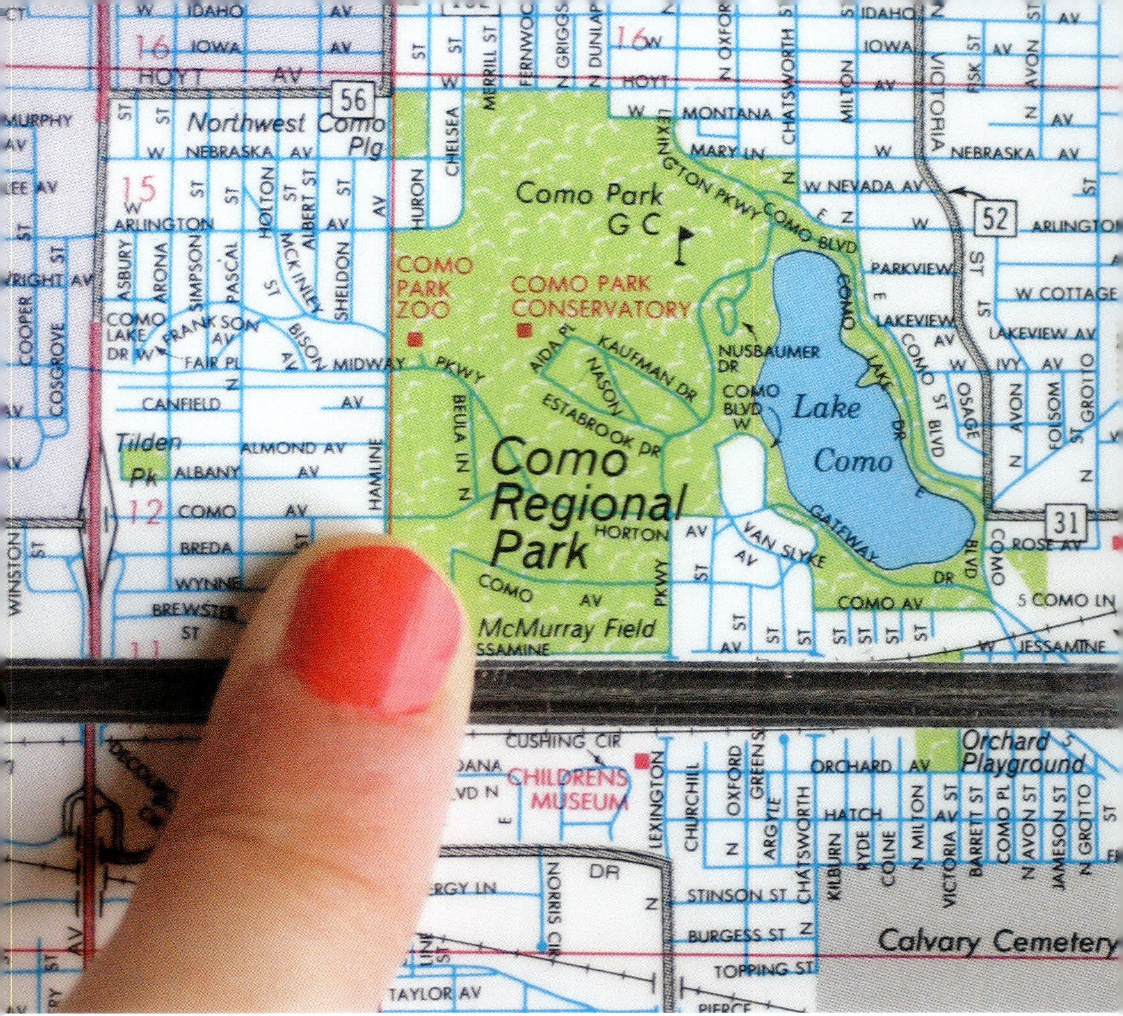
Northwest Como Plg
Como Park G C
COMO PARK ZOO
COMO PARK CONSERVATORY
Lake Como
Como Regional Park
McMurray Field
Tilden Pk
Orchard Playground
CHILDRENS MUSEUM
Calvary Cemetery
HOYT AV
IOWA AV
NEBRASKA AV
ARLINGTON AV
MIDWAY PKWY
CANFIELD AV
ALMOND AV
ALBANY AV
COMO AV
BREDA
HAMLINE
LEXINGTON PKWY
COMO BLVD
ESTABROOK DR
KAUFMAN DR
HORTON AV
VAN SLYKE AV
GATEWAY DR
VICTORIA ST
CHATSWORTH
ORCHARD AV
HATCH AV
STINSON ST
BURGESS ST
TOPPING ST
TAYLOR AV
56
52
31

Parks